After receiving a Grammar Sc... England, J. John Brand succeede... in History, French, and English ... ...u him to proceed to the University of London to read Medicine in the steps of his grandfather. He attended King's College Strand and Kings College Hospital Medical School, 1951–1597, receiving the Burridge Prize in 1956 and qualified L.R.C.P., M.R.C.S., 1956; and M.B., B.S., 1957. He was an enthusiastic hockey and cricket player. After some two years of internships in medicine, surgery, and paediatrics, he became liable for military service and elected to enter the Royal Navy as Acting Surgeon Lieutenant. He saw service in the Mediterranean, the Middle East, Indian Ocean and East Africa. Returning to the U.K., he began research at the Royal Naval Medical School under the aegis of the M.R.C. and R.N.P.R.C. and at a submarine base in the U.K. as MOSETT, and later served on fishery protection vessels in the North Atlantic. Having then developed an interest in the physiology and pharmacology of anti-motion sickness drugs, he left active service with the rank of Surgeon Lieutenant Commander, but pursued similar research activities in conjunction with the Dept. of Pharmacology, Edinburgh University, [Prof. W.L.M. Perry] supported by MRC Research grants, and afterwards at the R.A.F. Institute of Aviation, Farnborough. This led to the publication of various papers on allied subjects, and he proceeded to M.D. [Lond.] in 1968. He published a book, *Motion Sickness*, with Jim Reason, in 1975. After assisting in further hospital-based research on a different topic, involving the use of hyperbaric oxygen, he returned to full-time clinical work as a Primary Care Physician in Gosport Hants with a special interest in occupational medicine and remained there until retirement from full-time work. However, he has continued to maintain a clinical interest by doing locum work for the M.O.D. until fairly recent years.

LT. CHARLES BRAND, R.N., 1797–1872, BRITISH NAVAL OFFICER AND EXPLORER

Derring-Do in a Historical Setting

by

J. John Brand

AUSTIN MACAULEY PUBLISHERS™

LONDON • CAMBRIDGE • NEW YORK • SHARJAH

Copyright © J. John Brand (2019)

A CIP catalogue record for this title is available from the British Library.

ISBN 9781788781589 (Paperback)
ISBN 9781788781572 (Hardback)
ISBN 9781528955157 (ePub e-book)

www.austinmacauley.com

First Published (2019)
Austin Macauley Publishers Ltd
25 Canada Square
Canary Wharf
London
E14 5LQ

Dedicated to Pat O'Connor and the present-day descendants of Lieutenant Charles Brand, many of whom I have yet to meet, and any other connected members of the Brand family.

It is a great pleasure to acknowledge the assistance of the many librarians, archivists and individuals who have given advice and assistance in the preparation of this book. Although I feel it is somewhat invidious to single out individuals, I must thank Michael Tormey for sharing the portrait of Alexander Brand, 1756–1839, which had been lost to the family, and Jane Rowley Marsh for the portrait of Lt. G.R. Brand, as a 'Middy'. I must also mention my dear wife, Muriel, for her unfailing patience and help in the preparation of the work.

CONTENTS

Part 01 .... *11*
   Origins and Early Family Background _____ 12
   Charles Brand's Naval Career _____ 16
   The South Coast Blockade and the Wish Tower _____ 20
   St Helena and the South Atlantic _____ 25

Part 02 : **The Voyage to Peru** *33*
   Crossing the Andes on Foot During the Winter of 1828 ___ 34

Part 03 .... *43*
   Return to England and Search for Civilian Employment
   (1828–1834) _____ 44

Part 04 .... *47*
   Marriage in 1834, the Bath Years and Single Parenthood __ 48

Part 05 : **The Children of Charles Brand** *55*
   Louisa Georgina Brand _____ 56
   Commander Herbert Charles Alexander Brand, R.N. _____ 56
   Lieutenant Charles Rowley Brand, R.M. _____ 58
   William Horne Brand, 1844–1911 _____ 65
   The Rev. Hamilton Brand _____ 67
   And Finally, to Return to Charles Himself _____ 71

References *72*
Summary *73*

Part 01

Origins and Early Family Background

Lt. Charles Brand was born in Soho, Westminster, London, in 1797. He was the sixth son, but eighth child of Alexander Brand R.N. and his wife Ann Rallans, who were married in the church of St Martin in the Fields, Westminster, in April 1782. This marriage was arranged to acquire the special licence of the Bishop of London, but it is not clear why they should have needed this. It may be because of Alexander's previous Naval Service and Ann's residence in another parish at that time that the couple could not have suitable residential qualifications for the publication of Banns for a marriage to take place in a different parish or they might just have been following the prevailing fashion.

Alexander Brand (1756–1839) by Adam Buck, 1790

At the time of his birth, Charles had two sisters and five brothers. A few years after their marriage, the family came to reside at 14, Bateman's Buildings in the parish of St Ann's, Soho.

No image is now available as this building was, unfortunately, destroyed by Nazi air raids in WWII. So, an illustration of similar buildings of about the same period in nearby Frith St has been provided for interest and information.

Frith St, Soho, C 20

Bateman's Buildings was situated in a series of recently constructed apartments on land formerly owned by a Lord Bateman, which was, at that time, quite close to the open countryside to the North of Westminster, near the present-day Soho Square and Oxford St., only about two miles from the River Thames to the South.

Charles' father, Alexander, at that time described as a 'working jeweller', was of Scottish descent from the Brand

Family of Angus, with connections to the Brands of Baberton, a merchant and trading family in Edinburgh. As a landowning family, they had been obliged by old Scottish laws to register a Shield of Arms, back in 1680.

This was later to be used by Charles [Ref. The Brands of Baberton, 2009 and Thora's Archive]. Alexander was the son of Peter, a.k.a. Patrick Brand, a maltman in Dundee and Helen Martine and was baptised there, in May 1756.

Shield of Arms as used by Charles Brand

His grandfather, Robert Brand, was a wright (trade unspecified) and other members of the family were engaged in the clock and watchmakers trade in Edinburgh, at about this time. He is recorded as having been apprenticed as a hammerman in Dundee in 1771, to a master known as 'John Stiven' when about 15 years old, and paying dues of two shillings and four pence for the privilege, but there is no record of him completing his time and becoming a master himself. However, it would seem that he must have derived some benefit from his experience there as he subsequently became a working jeweller' some years later, down in London in about 1782.

Hammerman's entry, Dundee Archives, 1771

Exactly how or why he left Scotland remains obscure and is open to speculation, but there is the possibility that he subsequently joined the merchant service and later transferred to the R.N. or even that he was a victim of the Press Gangs active at that time, but this appears unlikely since there is some evidence that he had become a warrant officer in the Royal Navy by 1806 and should have enjoyed immunity from impressment as he was an indentured apprentice. At any rate, sometime after he arrived in London, he met Ann Rallans, born 1758, the eldest daughter of George Rallans and Elizabeth Norris, whom he married in April 1782. The Rallans family were merchants in Bishopsgate, City of London, and later resided in the parish of St Martin's, Westminster.

It was then that Alexander became a working jeweller residing in Soho, in the parish of St Anne's, but it is not known in which branch of the jewellery trade he specialised.

Interestingly enough, no record has been found of any London apprenticeship or membership of a City of London Guild, but this would not have been essential since he plied his trade outwith the boundaries of the 'City' and is known to have worked in Hatton Garden. How he acquired the necessary trade skills, therefore, remains obscure, but it has been suggested that with his previous naval connections, he might have been involved in the manufacture and ornamentation of commemorative swords and medals, but at about this time, he became a member of a masonic lodge for ex-naval personnel, situated in the docklands area, possibly through the agency of his new father-in-law.

Charles Brand's Naval Career

At the time of Charles' birth in May 1797, 14 Bateman's Buildings must have been quite a lively establishment with seven other children and their parents at the residence. The youngest of them, Thomas Dickson Brand, was only three years old at that time, but the eldest, Elizabeth Cecilia, was by then about 14 and no doubt could have acted as a second little mother to her siblings.

Shortly before his birth, in March of the same year, Charles' eldest brother George Rowley Brand would have already left home to enlist as a potential officer in the Royal Navy, as a 'Boy 2nd Class' on board H.M.S. Adamant, Capt. W. Hotham, then lying at Sheerness, overlooking the Medway and Thames Estuaries. His age on joining the ship was recorded as 16, but he was in fact only 13. This apparent advancement of age was a common practice in the Navy at the time; a promising recruit could not be promoted to the rank of lieutenant until he attained the nominal age of 18 years and had spent a number of years on the ship's books. This device, therefore, allowed for an earlier promotion, if his abilities proved it to be appropriate.

Lt. G.R. Brand (1784–1806) as a Middie. Buck, 1797

Regrettably, nothing is known of Charles' earlier education before he left home in 1810. He may have received private tuition, attended one of the local grammar schools or even one of the naval schools that existed in Greenwich and Portsmouth at that time, where preference for admission was given to candidates with family service connections. As a boy, he would be taken down to the Thames by his father to view the many vessels lying there in those days and was possibly inspired by his father's accounts of naval life.

Charles' naval career is described in considerable detail by O' Byrne in the Naval Biographical Dictionary (1849), which also describes that of his elder brother William Henry Brand, born in 1790.

Charles Brand Service Record (entry to discharge)

Charles himself entered the Navy in 1810, at the age of 13. By this time, his brother, who had already entered the Service some five years previously in 1805, had found himself in action as a midshipman on board H.M.S. Revenge at the Battle of Trafalgar only four months after joining his first ship.

Charles entered the Service as a 'Volunteer First Class', on board the 'Apelles', 14 guns, Captains Thomas Oliver and Fred Hoffman, which was at that time in the Channel Station, and was soon involved in action himself. On 5th May 1812, the vessel was run on shore near Boulogne, but he was fortunate enough to escape capture by the French, along with several others, by taking timely flight in the ship's boats. He was then posted to Bermuda as a midshipman in the troopship 'Ardent', where he joined the 'Majestic', a cut-down 74, Captain John Hayes. He was next involved in the capture of the French frigate 'Terpsichore', after a running battle of two and a half hours and the capture of a large number of American prizes, which must have been of great benefit to his bank balance. He took part in the capture of Washington and witnessed the surrender of the 'President' to the 'Endymion'. From 1815–1818, he served on the 'Caledonia', 120, Captain Sir Archibald Collingwood Dickson, and then on the 'Rochfort', 80, at Plymouth, and after this as admiralty midshipman on the 'Queen Charlotte', 100, at Portsmouth.

HMS Queen Charlotte in Portsmouth Harbour, 1870

Figurehead (2004)

HMS Queen Charlotte's Figurehead in 2004

The South Coast Blockade and the Wish Tower

From 1818–1820, Charles was employed in the South Coast Blockade for the Prevention of Smuggling. It had been established by a Captain McCulloch at the beginning of the 19th century, but by 1818, it had become evident that it needed to be extended in order to remain effective. Charles himself wrote an amusing and informative contemporary account of his experiences in a book called *The Merry Middies of the Enchantress*, which finally came to be published many years later in a collection of naval adventure stories.

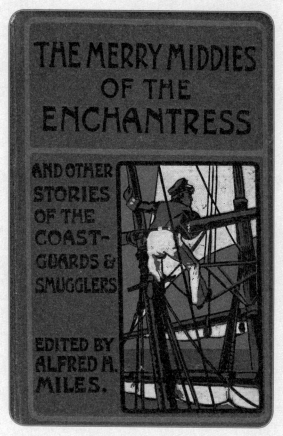

Merry Middies book cover

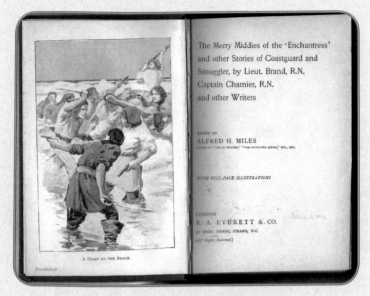

The Merry Middies of the 'Enchantress'
and other Stories of Coastguard and
Smuggler, by Lieut. Brand, R.N.
Captain Chamier, R.N.
and other Writers

EDITED BY
ALFRED H. MILES

WITH FULL-PAGE ILLUSTRATIONS

LONDON
R. A. EVERETT & CO.
47 ESSEX STREET, STRAND, W.C.
[All Rights Reserved.]

A FIGHT ON THE BEACH.

Merry Middies Frontispiece and Title Page

Although now being many years out of print, J. J. B. is fortunate enough to possess a copy from which the following extracts have been derived. Charles described himself as one of the "thoughtless and happy class of youngsters termed 'midshipmen', whose ambition and love of the Service were kept alive by the flattery of their senior officers holding out to them prospects of being future admirals and Heroes of the Navy."

He was sent to Deal from the 'Queen Charlotte' with 100 others to join the 'Severn' and from there with a further 50 Middies, to board the 'Enchantress', which was to become a depot and headquarters ship in the little harbour at Rye on the South coast.

Unfortunately, she managed to arrive off Rye on the last of the tide, which was then ebbing at the rate of some four knots, so that she grounded before she could reach the dock, which had been newly prepared for her. The result was that she tipped over on her beam ends and half-filled with water, thus setting all her midshipmen's gear afloat in the hold.

This led to a frantic rush to save their personal property

and convey it safely ashore, over half a mile of soft mud to a neighbouring inn at the harbour mouth. Charles describes how they were "scattered over the mud like a horde of gypsies dragging their chests and trunks with towlines, frequently sinking up to their knees, leaving a diversity of toggery [sic] scattered over the beach in all directions: cocked hats, boots, shoes, coats, shirts all spread out to dry."

All this was apparently to the great entertainment of the local inhabitants. However, in two days' time, by which the ship was properly docked and upright again, they were given appointments up and down the coast to various Martello towers.

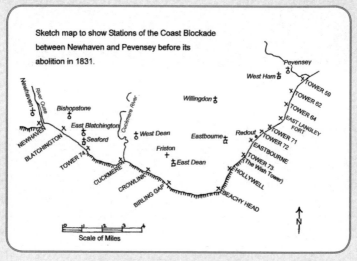

Martello Towers, sketch map

These were defensive structures built some years earlier and named after similar structures in the Mediterranean. He describes them as being "like dungeons with only two small windows, which barely admitted any light through the walls, which were some 12 feet thick. The inside of the tower was wet and damp with mildew and had to be cleaned out."

The Wish Tower (Tower 73) Eastbourne

They then had to look after themselves and do their own cooking and cleaning etc., but it appears that they quite enjoyed the novelty of being their own masters and servants. They were then put under the command of a naval lieutenant and had to patrol the shoreline and adjacent coast during the hours of darkness in both summer and winter, visiting 'sentinels', who were posted up and down the coast and were on the look-out for smugglers.

The sentinels who were recruited from various sources, did not prove very trustworthy and were quite liable to have been bribed by the smugglers. However, it would appear that for the most part the smugglers tried to avoid violence, unless actually caught handling contraband and found it preferable to disappear quietly into the darkness, to avoid capture and any subsequent criminal proceedings and punishment.

Charles was involved in fights from time to time and did receive some unpleasant injuries, but fortunately, no gunshot wounds, though he did have some near misses. He was also subjected to threats, one of which he quotes from a letter 'written in a disguised hand',

"Sir, you had better not be so harde upon us, for if you do, we will knok out your branes the furst time we ketch you alone in the dark and we will kill your dog."

In this respect, he was more fortunate than two of his contemporaries, a lieutenant and a midshipman, who were ambushed by the smugglers and shot dead at about this time. He did, however, make several successful seizures of contraband, on one occasion getting 228 tubs of spirits and sundry bales of tea and tobacco, for which he received a reward of 100£ from the government.

The significance of this sum can be appreciated when it is compared with the average annual wage for a midshipman of about £ 26. The Coast Blockade was later to be abolished in 1831, and a good account of its activities was written and published by Rosemary Milton in 1991, for the Eastbourne and District Family History Society.

St Helena and the South Atlantic

On 18 June 1820, Charles was appointed to H.M.S. Shearwater at Chatham where she was fitting out for the Cape of Good Hope and St Helena Station, and she sailed on 29th July for this destination. He then remained on 'Shearwater' during the time of the imprisonment of Napoleon Bonaparte on this island and while serving on board, he is reported to have helped while away the time of the exile by playing chess with him. This information is drawn from the memoirs of his cousin, Frances Henderson, who was the daughter of his elder brother Captain William Henry Brand, R.N. and whose diary was published many years later, in 1968.

He then sailed for the Cape in H.M.S. Heron, and while on this station was given command of the Government Vessel 'Henrietta', which was carrying out patrols for the suppression of slavery on the authority of the Governor of Mauritius. While in this part of the world, he also travelled in Namaqualand which was then a little known and unexplored part of the country.

He is said to have written an account of his experiences there, but regrettably, no published record of his adventures can be found, and a search for this has defeated the best efforts of the British Library, the Royal Geographical Society and the National Library of Congress.

However, some idea of the hazards he faced can be found in the following extract from the family papers, contained in a letter written by Benson Burchett to his niece, 'Babs' (Thora Brand's sister), around 1935 [Ref. Thora Brand's Archive, unpublished]:

"Some explorer was lost in the North Part of South Africa and the government of the day ordered your Great grand papa to organise a search party and discover the missing man. A great part of the country was unknown land then and the search party fared worse than the explorer, whom they could not find. Finally, food and water gave out and death by thirst, hunger and exhaustion seemed imminent.

"Fortunately, they were near the coast and one of the niggers [sic] attached to the party carried your great grandpapa pickaback down to the shore, and he had the great good luck to find a vessel cruising not far out. They sighted him and the nigger and took them aboard. It wasn't a part of the coast where there was much traffic, and your great grandpapa had reason to be thankful for that nigger and that ship."

[It should be noted that the term 'nigger' was in common usage at that time as a derivative from the Latin term 'niger', simply meaning a 'black man', and not in any sense derogatory or pejorative as it has since unfortunately become].

Charles was confirmed as Lieutenant on the Cygnet, on 21 December 1822, having passed the examination for this rank some years earlier. When the ship paid off on 22 April 1823, he was presented with an elegant sword 'in testimony of his gentlemanly and officer-like conduct while on board'. He was then again appointed to the Coast Blockade in April 1824 and was retained in the Service, but on half-pay from August 1825. His intentions at that time are not clear. However, with the earlier cessation of hostilities with France and America and the exile and death of Napoleon Bonaparte, the threat to his homeland was greatly diminished. This could have meant the end of his naval career as the Navy again contracted and any prospects of advancement had been greatly reduced, as many former naval officers found themselves 'on the beach'. Although he had returned to the Coast Blockade for a short period, this was shortly to be abolished.

Charles Brand newly commissioned as Lieutenant, RN
ca.1822, artist unknown

As regards to the other members of his family, his eldest brother, Lt. George Rowley Brand had been killed in action against the French at in 1806 and buried ashore with full military honours. The second brother, John Alexander Brand had remained in civilian life and carried on the family traditions as a merchant.

John Alexander Brand, ca. 1825

Another older brother Lt. William Henry Brand entered the Coast Guard in 1825, and served in the Shetlands, where he met his wife, Christina Grieg. They later moved to Leigh-on-Sea, Essex, where he continued to serve in the Coast Guard until his death in 1860.

A younger brother, Lt. Thomas Dickson Brand, was still in the Navy and present at the siege of Rangoon in 1824, but unfortunately was to contract a chronic and severe illness there which meant that he had to leave the Service and return home to live with his parents in Charlotte St., London, until his death in 1830 at the early age of 36.

Lt. Thomas Dickson Brand, RN

No.5, Charlotte St., Bloomsbury, C 20

His brother Major James Brand of the Bedfordshire Regiment continued to serve in India until he returned to England later that century. Therefore, it was against a somewhat changing and unsettled background that Charles undertook his voyage to Peru in 1828.

Major James Brand, 1789–1865

Part 02

The Voyage to Peru

Crossing the Andes on Foot During the Winter of 1828

It seems possible that life outwith the Royal Navy did not appear sufficiently stimulating or rewarding for Charles after his previous adventures in the Service, which may have been why he came to embark on the voyage to Peru. It is not, however, known what prompted him to undertake this enterprise or how it was financed.

Charles gives a fascinating and detailed account of his journey to South America in 1827 and 1828 which was published in London on his return in 1828. He crossed the Andes in the winter (i.e. August in the Southern Hemisphere) and returned in the summer the following January.

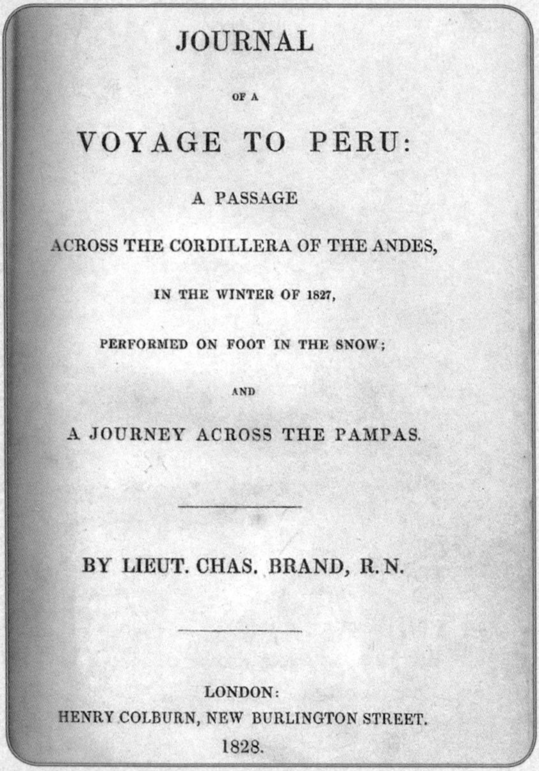

JOURNAL

OF A

VOYAGE TO PERU:

A PASSAGE

ACROSS THE CORDILLERA OF THE ANDES,

IN THE WINTER OF 1827,

PERFORMED ON FOOT IN THE SNOW;

AND

A JOURNEY ACROSS THE PAMPAS.

BY LIEUT. CHAS. BRAND, R.N.

LONDON:
HENRY COLBURN, NEW BURLINGTON STREET.
1828.

Title page of Charles B's book, 1828

Ascending the Cumbre of the Andes

Travelling on the Pampas with a relay of horses

Descending the Cuesta de Concual in the
Cordillera of the Andes

The reasons for this expedition are obscure; whether they were political, geographical or scientific—they are unknown at the present time, along with his source of funding. A query to the National Archives has been non-productive. It is difficult to believe that it was a purely private venture and this would surely have been quite beyond the means of a naval lieutenant on half-pay. There remains, therefore, the suggestion of some kind of official or a possible clandestine government sponsorship, but no evidence of this has been found so far.

He states in the introduction to the book published in 1828, "I will not detain my readers with any account of the nature or objects of the mission on which I was employed," which is, of course, very frustrating to those of us who would really like to know. Later on in the account of his adventures, when he had arrived in Lima, he wrote that he "received orders to return to England", [p.179] but does not mention the source of these 'orders', and there is further evidence in the narrative of some degree of urgency to make the return journey.

Reading between the lines, the story he tells may perhaps be considered to give several insights into his own character, personality and susceptibilities. There is evidence of a deep and sincere Christian belief and trust in Providence, no doubt engendered by his previous experiences at sea and ashore in Namaqualand and then reinforced by later events. As he remarked, "Would sailors but reflect, then would they acknowledge the wonders of the Lord".

He was clearly pleased to find that an encouraging degree of religious tolerance was prevalent in Buenos Aires and wrote of his admiration for the religious music he heard in the Cathedral at Lima, but expressed regret at the conduct of some of the priests there which sadly seems to have left a lot to be desired [pp.189, 190].

There is further evidence of an enquiring and scientific turn of mind due to his collection of samples of water gathered locally, which were later sent to be analysed by the distinguished scientist, Faraday, in London on his return. It also shows in his unsuccessful attempt to acquire the severed head of an executed robber, for subsequent examination by a phrenologist of his acquaintance, no doubt to see whether it showed any characteristic criminal features! [p.264]

It is intriguing and somewhat puzzling to read of his revulsion at what he terms the "disgusting" dress of the ladies of Lima [p.182], and why did he find it so disgusting? It appeared to him to reflect their moral depravity in some way, but since they were virtually covered from head to toe in their walking-out dress as shown in his drawing, it is difficult to appreciate this in the 21st Century. Of course, this would have been their

'Sunday Best' and might have been somewhat different from their every-day wear, which is not illustrated. Perhaps it was due to the contrast with what would have been fashionable in Western Europe at that time and would have been interesting to speculate as to what his mother and sisters back in London would have been wearing. He was clearly appalled by the sight of ladies smoking cigars [p.176 and 177] or was this written somewhat tongue-in-cheek? The illustrations by the author gives evidence of accurate observation and considerable artistic ability.

A Lady of Lima in her walking dress

Another fascinating feature of the narrative was his tendency, in the later part of the book, to illustrate his point by suddenly quoting some lines of verse, which appear highly appropriate and were presumably of his own composition since there is no other acknowledgment as to their authorship. These were written in the style which was fashionable at that time and first appear in Chapter 8, when he describes the misfortune of the Roberton brothers who were shipwrecked in a storm. The squall which caused the destruction of their ship is described in this stanza:

"And swift and fatal as the lightning's course,

Thro' the torn main-sail burst with thund'ring force."

More verses appear a little later when Charles is relating his own hazardous experiences in a storm when returning from Lima to Valparaiso; a further poetic description is given of his thoughts at sea, on observing the increasing declination of the Pole Star when travelling north from the equator with the realisation that this meant that he was homeward-bound and that he would soon be back in England [p.309]. This ability to compose such appropriate lines of verse would appear to be yet another example of his many and varied talents.

He gives a great deal of practical advice to other potential travellers, together with some interesting comments on the preservation of their general health. Although he admits to not being a medical man, he draws again on his past experiences in what he describes as his 'servitude in the Navy'. Some of this advice is somewhat alarming to present-day eyes, viz. "Previous to taking a journey across the Pampas (or anywhere in the interior of a foreign country) the traveller is advised to take 5 grains of calomel [a salt derived from mercury!] at night and a dose of Epsom salts the following morning, which will carry off any excrementitious matter that may be lodged in the bowels." Since 5 grains in the old apothecary units equals to approximately 300 mg in present-day metric notation [i.e. some 3 times the usual adult dose], with the addition of the Epsom salts, there is little doubt as to the dramatic effect which would have been produced and might have prevented comfortable travel for some time afterwards.

Also somewhat disconcerting is the advice given on the benefits of bloodletting from a suitable vein, to 'unload distended blood vessels' and relieve headaches, fortunately with instructions as to how to avoid an artery. The subject of frostbites is covered [p.133] with extensive quotations from a contemporary medical author on the effects of cold [p.120]. Protective clothing was to be a "complete suit of flannel next to the skin" covered by soft leather, the equivalent of modern thermal underwear.

He was obviously puzzled by the occurrence of 'mountain sickness', known locally as "puna", but doesn't seem to have been much troubled by it himself. Although it is now understood, from the work of subsequent pioneer scientists, that this condition is directly related to the low partial pressure of oxygen found in inspired air at high altitudes and to cerebral oedema, he obviously would have had no means of appreciating this and, therefore, put it down to the presence of 'unfamiliar minerals in the ground'. Perhaps he didn't attempt much bloodletting, just before crossing the Andes at high altitudes, or his own personal experience of 'puna' might have been somewhat more dramatic.

No record has been found to suggest that Charles received any recognition or remuneration for his exertions in South America, and he simply suggested that it was written "according to a very general custom amongst naval officers, solely for the information and amusement of my friends, without any view to publication". However, he was later "persuaded to present it to the notice of the public, in the hope that it might be found to contain some information useful to those whose business or pleasure may lead them to pursue the paths which I have so recently trodden".

Part 03

Return to England and Search for Civilian Employment (1828–1834)

After his return from South America, Charles contacted several of his former superior officers, including Captain W. H. Dickson. He also sought the support of Lord Gambier, a former naval officer of distinction, who had in fact flown his flag in the 'Prince of Wales' as Admiral in Charge of the Siege of Copenhagen in 1807.

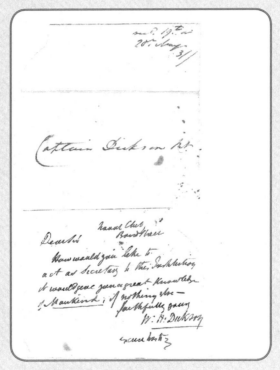

Letter from Capt. W.H. Dickson to Charles Brand, 1831

It is thought that Charles' father, Alexander, might possibly also have served with Gambier at the Siege of Copenhagen (according to a memo written later by his grandson George) or that there was some earlier family connection which led him make this approach, but this is yet to be clarified.

Whatever the case, Charles received a helpful letter from Gambier and subsequently obtained the post of Secretary at the Royal Naval School. It is clear that Charles maintained various other naval contacts at this time and he is recorded as having lent books to an admiral of his acquaintance, Admiral Nugent, in 1832.

Letter from Gambier to Charles Brand, 1828

Also at about the same time, his parents, now both just turned 70, together with his sister Elizabeth, had moved from 14, Bateman's Buildings to a comfortable residence at 5, Charlotte St., Bloomsbury and he was living with them. Furthermore, his eldest brother, John Alexander, married Elizabeth Hudson at their parish church, St George's Bloomsbury. His brother William Henry Brand had moved up to the Shetlands, as mentioned above, where he was to meet and later marry Christina Greig, the daughter of the local Procurator Fiscal.

Another brother Lt. Thomas Dickson Brand had left the Navy by this time and returned to the parental home, having served in India and been present at the Siege of Rangoon in 1824. Unfortunately, he had contracted some debilitating tropical illness there and since it is recorded that there was a severe outbreak of cholera among the troops and seamen, it is possible that it was this which was to lead to his death in November 1830 at the early age of 36.

Another brother James Brand, now aged 40, was at that time a Captain in the 16th Regiment of Foot, then serving in India at Bengal, and had married Harriet Phipps, the daughter of Robert Phipps of Demerara, at St George's Church, Madras in 1827.

The house at 5, Charlotte St is still standing, but the lower floor and frontage have been modified and put to various uses over the years. A few years ago, it had become a restaurant. So, J. J. B., together with M. P. B., knowing the past history of the building, went to have a meal there; so we actually had the opportunity of dining in what had been the former family residence in London.

Part 04

Marriage in 1834, the Bath Years and Single Parenthood

It appears that Charles eventually tired of the wandering, adventurous bachelor life and on 20 December 1834, at the age of 37, he married Caroline Julia Sanders, who was some 20 years his junior and the daughter of the late Joseph Sanders of Great Portland St., London, who had died on 19 March 1833, aged 53. The wedding took place at St Margaret's, Westminster and was presumably a rather grand affair, although no report of the event has been located so far.

How long the couple remained in London is not known, but their first child, Louisa Georgina, was born in Bath on 6 August 1836, when their address is given as 'Canal House, Bath,' and Charles is recorded as being a 'Lieutenant, R.N.' This suggests the possibility that he might have been given an appointment in connection with the Waterways Association and the newly developed Kennet and Avon Canal connecting Bath to London, but no other firm evidence of this has come to light so far, though further weight is given to this theory by the fact that their place of residence is listed as 'Canal Office' in the birth records of his later children.

With reference to the Canal House, Bath, the following details were kindly provided by Sarah Gould and Caroline Jones of the Kennet and Avon Canal Trust and the Waterways Trust. Although generally known as 'Cleveland House', it first appeared on town maps in 1825, as 'Canal House'. It is a 3-storey, Palladian-style stone house built over a canal tunnel entrance. Originally built for Henry Duke of Cleveland, it later became the original headquarters of the Kennet and Avon Canal company. In 1864, the canal's affairs were transferred by the GWR to a central administration at Paddington, London, and the old Canal Office at Cleveland House was let to a tenant at £75 p.a. from 1865. Interestingly enough, it was being modified for re-sale as apartments in 2016.

Canal House, Bath, view of frontage

Canal House, Bath, back view

Following the birth of Louisa Georgina, the couple had four more children, all of them boys and born during their residence there, viz:

- Herbert Charles Alexander Brand, later Commander, R.N. (1839–1901),
- Charles Rowley Brand, later Lieutenant, Royal Marines, (1841–1864),
- William Horne Brand, (1844–1911), who later joined the Indian Civil Service, and
- Hamilton Brand, later Rector of Barningham, (1848–1931).

Regrettably, in spite of what might have appeared to be a pleasant retreat to the rural tranquillity and elegant beauties of the ancient city of Bath with its Roman foundations, and with what was probably a not too demanding source of employment for Charles, life did not run smoothly for the couple. Perhaps the rural situation and lifestyle did not suit Caroline after her youthful upbringing in fashionable London and it has now been revealed, from family papers, that she actually eloped with a lover (identity not reported) not long after the birth of their youngest child, Hamilton, in 1848, after some 14 years of marriage.

It is not known exactly what became of Caroline after she deserted her husband and young family, but a record has recently been found of the marriage of a 'Caroline Julia Brand' in 1872 (ref. Kensington 1a, 391,), who it is thought might have become Charles' widow shortly before this and wished to regularise her previous relationship.

Bath 1851 Census

This obviously left Charles with serious problems as a single parent family. The eldest being a girl of about 14, could perhaps have helped out with her young brothers. However, further assistance was to be found from his eldest unmarried sister, Elizabeth Cecilia, although 65 and living with her widowed mother in London. The 1851 census reveals that she must have been able to move to Bath, where she is recorded as living with him and the two younger boys, aged six and four and three domestic servants.

The two older boys were not mentioned, but as they were both destined for military careers were thought to be away at school, H.C.A. at the R.N. school at Deptford, and C.R. elsewhere. The subsequent fate of Charles' family and their involvement in the events of their times was also to prove colourful and of great interest.

After the crisis had been averted to some extent, Elizabeth Cecilia returned to London to live in Islington with her youngest brother, Ferdinand Brand, a solicitor with the Corporation of the City of London, who was later to act as Charles's attorney after his death, until her death in December 1865. Interestingly enough, she remembered the Bath family in her will, leaving £100 to her brother Charles, £25 to Louisa Georgina and £10 to her nephew Hamilton, as well as bequests to various other members of the family.

Ferdinand's appointment as an attorney to Charles p.1

ratifying and confirming and agreeing to ratify and confirm
all and whatsoever the said Ferdinand Brand shall lawfully
do or cause to be done in or about the premises aforesaid In
Witness whereof I the said Charles Brand have hereunto
set my hand and seal the   day of September
one thousand eight hundred and forty five.

Signed Sealed and Delivered
by the above named Charles
Brand in the presence of

Ferdinand's appointment as an attorney to Charles p.2

Part 05

The Children of Charles Brand

Louisa Georgina Brand

Born in 1836, Louisa appears in the census of 1841, aged 5 years, living in Bath with her parents and brother Herbert. There is no mention of her in Bath in the 1851 census, for she was apparently away at Little Green, the R.N. School in Richmond, Surrey. She reappears in 1861, now aged 25, with her father Charles, 63, and brother William Horne, aged 16. As mentioned below, she had moved back to London with her father by 1871, but it has not so far been possible to trace her after this record in the census of 1871. Recently been discovered that she married George Windsor, watchmaker, on 23 June 1880, at Harrismith, OFS, S. Africa. [P.C. Robin Comley, 2017.]

Commander Herbert Charles Alexander Brand, R.N.

Thanks to the censuses and various other sources, a fairly complete picture can be built up of his life and movements. Interestingly enough, although later christened at Bath, he was actually born in Boulogne, France, but why the family was there at that time is not known. By 1851, he had become a pupil at the R.N. School at Counter Hill, St Paul's, Deptford.

He then entered the R.N. and in the census of 1861, we find him serving as a lieutenant on board the 'Royal Adelaide' which appears to have been a training vessel and was in Devonport at that time. Later in the 1860s, he served in the West Indies and was unfortunate enough to achieve a certain amount of notoriety at a time of civil unrest in Jamaica.

As Uncle Benson was to put it in his letter to Lilith (Babs), "He was the Naval Officer in Command in Jamaican waters when a riot broke out among the niggers [sic] in the island…. The Governor General of the Island whose name was Eyre consulted your great-uncle and the result was that a landing party was put ashore in [his] command, but as the riot continued, the order to fire was given and some of the rioters were killed. John Bright, who was a quaker [and] a great political figure in this country at the time…insisted on Governor Eyre and your great-uncle being tried at the Old Bailey...the alleged crime was 'needless bloodshed'. The trial caused a great sensation in its day. Of course the Governor and your great uncle were acquitted." [ref. Brand, H.C.A., Charge of the Lord Chief Justice of England in the cause of the Queen against Nelson and Brand, 1867, British Library.]

Captain de Horsey was the Admiral Algernon Frederick Rous de Horsey, the dates of whose commissions, etc., will be found in the Flag Officers' List. Lieutenant Herbert Charles Alexander Brand, commanding the *Onyx*, one of the smallest of the gunboats which had been built for the purposes of the war with Russia, became a victim of a hot and foolish agitation in England, the result of which was that, with Brigadier-General Nelson, he was arraigned at the Old Bailey on a charge of wilful murder. The prisoners were happily acquitted; and, after further honourable service, Brand retired in 1883 with the rank of Commander. He died in 1901.

Herbert Charles Alexander Brand, acquitted of murder

However, Herbert appears to have recovered from this ordeal sufficiently to get married on August 19 of that year, back at his family's parish, in the Parish Church of Bathwick, Bath. His wife was Rosa Straghan (probably pronounced 'Strawn'), who also hailed from an old Scottish family and her father, the Rev. Abel Andrew Straghan, who was the vicar there, married the couple. One of the witnesses, possibly the brother of the bride, signed himself 'A. Strachan, Captain in the 747th Highlanders'. [ref. For the Marriage is Bath, Avon, Somerset 1867, 5c, 969] Their eldest son, another Herbert, was born 3 May 1868 at Netley, Hants.

Herbert is next found in London in 1871, at 241, Vauxhall Bridge Road, London described as a 'Lieutenant R.N.' on the Active List, together with Rosa, his wife, and their two small children, 'Bertie', now aged 2, and Alice aged 1, together with one servant. By 1881, they had moved to Regent St., but there is now no mention of Alice and it is known that Bertie was away at Brook House School in Bedfordshire.

Following the family's military tradition, Bertie later went to Sandhurst and was subsequently commissioned in the

Highland Light Infantry to serve in India, in the India Staff Corps. The family later moved down to Bath. Herbert Charles Alexander retired with the rank of Commander and, in 1891, is recorded as living there with his youngest son, Cecil, who was then aged 10. He remained there until 1901 at 8, Bathwick Hill, where, shortly before he died, he was visited by Bertie, who was by then promoted to Captain in the Highland Light Infantry and home on leave from the India Staff Corps. His younger son Cecil was at that time commissioned in the Lancashire Fusiliers and serving in South Africa at the time of the Boer Wars.

Lieutenant Charles Rowley Brand, R.M.

Details of Charles Rowley's early education are not known and the first record of his independent life shows that he was commissioned as a Second Lieutenant Royal Marines in May 1859. According to Uncle Benson Burchett in his letter to Lilith (Babs), he saw service in China in the Opium Wars at about this time, but was promoted to First Lieutenant on 15 December 1861 while on board H.M.S. Immortalite, then lying off the Rio Grande.

This was just before the outbreak of the American Civil War. At this time, the Confederate States were anxious to recruit experienced officers for their Navy and, thus, it came about that he was discharged from his ship in March 1863, as he volunteered to undertake two years loan service in the Confederate States Navy.

Charles R. Brand, extract from Further Orders ref. SO279

S. O. 279. Oct 14 / 63.

XIII Mr. Charles R. Brand is hereby di-
-rected to report to Com Leon Smith for
duty in the Marine Dep't with the pay
and emoluments of a Capt of Marines
until the action of Lt Genl Smith
Com'g the Trans Miss Department
or of the Sec of war is made known
to these Head Quarters —   C.P.T.

Extract from US Civil War Veterans' Records SO279

In October of the same year, he was appointed as Captain and Executive Officer of the gunboat 'Sachem', which had been recently captured from the Federal States at the battle of Sabine Pass. Although quite severely damaged, she was speedily repaired and put back into service to operate out of Galveston and Sabine Pass, Texas in support of the army. Unfortunately, he did not enjoy his command for very long because the following year he contracted yellow fever. This was to prove fatal and he died at Sabine Pass on 8 January 1864, as reported in the Naval and Military Gazette on 12 March. A query has been sent to the Texas Historical Commission with regards to the possibility of any relevant M.I. (Monumental Inscription) and enquiries have recently been made locally by my distant cousin Don Brand, a retired U.S.M.C. aviator and resident in Missouri, but it seems likely that any M.I. might have been lost or vandalised.

Gunboat Sachem, 1860

After his death some of Charles Rowley's possessions found their way to the house of his younger brother Hamilton at Barningham Rectory, Norfolk, and remained there for some time.

According to his Uncle Benson, amongst his possessions were his portrait, that of a clean-shaven, dark-haired man in his 20s; his red jacket, which smelled strongly of tobacco, and his military sword bearing a stain said to have been acquired by running a Chinaman through the liver in the opium wars. *However, it was more probably a rust-mark acquired somewhat later,* thought Uncle Benson, *because no self-respecting marine officer would allow a stain to remain on his sword.*

The loss of his son must have been shattering news for Charles. He received a letter dated 13 May 1865 from a naval secretary named William Terry who was at that time on board the steamer 'Camargo' off the Rio Grande, but had been unable to write earlier because of the U.S. Coastal Blockade.

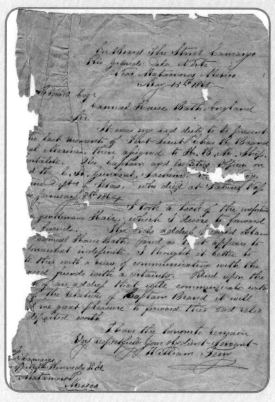

First letter from William Terry, 1865

Transcript of Letter 1 from William Terry.

(With original spelling etc.)

On Board The Stmr Camargo
Rio Grande Dela Norte
Near Matamoros Mexico
May 13th.1865

Brand Esqr.

Cannal House, Bath, England

Sir

It was my sad duty to be present *(?in /at)* the last moments of First Lieut.Charles R Brand *(Ro)*yal Marines, then assigned to H. B. M. Ship. *(Immo)*rtalité. Also Captain and Executive Officer on *(boar)*d the C.St. Gunboat, Sachem, *(? Confederate Navy,* *Marin)*e Dept^{mt} of Texas,   who died at Sabine Pass *(Tex)*as January 8th. 1864.

I took a lock of the **unfortunate** *(youn)*g Gentlemans Hair, which I desire to forward *(to hi)*s friends.   The only address I could obtain *(wa)*s Cannal House Bath, and as that appears to *(be)* somewhat indefinite, I thought it better to *(wri)*te this with a view of communicating with the *(dece)*ased*(ʼs?)* friends with a certainty.   And upon the *(receip)*t of an address that will communicate with *(any)* of the relatives of Captain Brand it will *(affor)*d me great pleasure to forward this sad relic *(of)* departed worth

I have the honour to Remain

Very Respectfully Your obedient Servant

William Terry

*(Addr)*ess
*(Stm)*r Camargo
*((Ca)*re of)* Messrs Kennedy & Co.
Matamoros   Mexico

Transcript of first letter from William Terry

He had been present at Charles Rowley's death and stated that he had taken a lock of his hair which he wished to forward to his next of kin, as was the custom at that time, but thought that 'Canal house, Bath' was too indefinite a location and so he requested confirmation of the address. This appears to have been at about the time that Charles was leaving Bath to return to London, because it was actually his son Hamilton who replied to William Terry in July of that year. Terry then wrote back on

22 September to Hamilton (at that time residing at 3, Sussex Villas Richmond), forwarding the lock of hair, and apologising for the delay in doing so, which was because of the United States Coastal Blockade.

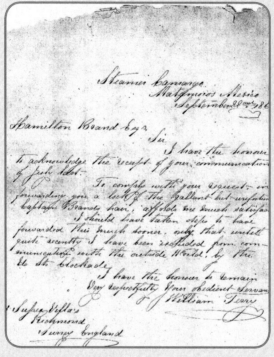

Second letter from William Terry re. Charles Rowley Brand

Transcript of Letter 2 from William Terry.

(With original spelling etc.)

Steamer Camargo

Matamoros Mexico

September 22nd.1865

Hamilton Brand Esqr.

Sir

I have the honour
to acknowledge the receipt of your communication
of July last.

To comply with your request, in
forwarding you a lock of the gallant but unfortunate
Captain Brands Hair, affords me much satisfaction

I should have taken steps to have
forwarded this much sooner, only that until
quite recently I have been excluded from communication with the outside World ,   by   the
U   Sts blockade

I have the honour to Remain

Very Respectfully Your obedient Servant

William Terry

3 Sussex Villa's

Richmond

Surrey England

Transcript of second letter

It seems that it is not generally appreciated that Great Britain gave a large measure of support to the Confederate States in this conflict, probably for reasons of trade. Following the election of President Lincoln in 1860, the Southern States were not prepared to accept a Republican Government dedicated to the abolition of slavery on which their economy was largely dependent. They were at a considerable disadvantage in terms of manpower materials and arms production for any subsequent hostilities. Also, the North was able to blockade the Southern Ports and thus, strangle all trade, which led to the South turning to Europe for help.

An agent was sent to Liverpool to negotiate in 1861 [ref.

Ghost Ships of the Mersey, Williams K. J.]. Several ships were then built secretly at Liverpool and they subsequently inflicted very considerable damage on the United States Navy and merchantmen. Britain, although nominally a neutral country, also allowed the South the use of ports and facilities. After the War, this led to the 'Alabama Claim' made by the North, as the British Government was alleged to have been in breach of International Law by supporting the South. An international arbitration commission was set up and, in 1873, Britain had to pay £3 million in compensation.

William Horne Brand, 1844–1911

Born in Bath in November 1844, he appears in the 1851 census as 'Scholar, aged 6' and ten years later as 'Scholar, aged 16', still resident at Bath. He may well have been away at school during this period, but perhaps was on holiday in Bath at the time the census was taken. Interestingly enough, we also know that he was confirmed at about this time, by the Lord Bishop of Oxford, at St John's Parochial Chapel, Eton, on 19 March 1862 and we have a Certificate for this signed by one Lambart Edwards, Vicar of Dornay, Bucks. This raises the possibility of attendance at Eton College at this period, but this has not been confirmed.

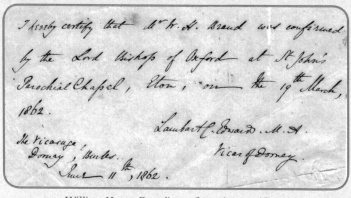

William Horne Brand's confirmation certificate

He received an appointment to the Indian Civil Service as an 'accountant fourth grade' in July 1869 and worked with the Indian Railways. He enlisted with the Freemasons in the Ravee Lodge, Lahore, in September 1870, married his first wife, Frances Payne, on 16 November 1872, at what was then called Bombay (now Mumbai) and became established as an 'examiner' in the North West Province, in 1876, serving in various regions of the country over the next 20 years.

After being allowed 18 months furlough in December 1886, he returned to India for a relatively short period but returned to England in 1891. He was by that time a widower, his profession being recorded in the census of that year as 'Indian Civil Service' and was staying as a visitor to the Rev. Charles Quicke, Rector of Ashbrittle and family, at Rectory House, Bath. He subsequently married Rachel Edwards [ref. Thetford 4b 1047, Oct, Nov. Dec.], daughter of the Rev. James Edwards, (sometime Vicar of Barningham) and sister of the Rev. Arthur Edwards, who succeeded James to the living at Barningham and was in turn succeeded by Hamilton Brand in 1903.

In 1901, he is described as 'Retired Examiner to the Indian Civil Service', living at 46, Blomfield Rd. in the parish of St Saviour's, Paddington, London, together with his wife Rachel, then aged 54, with two servants, a cook and parlour maid. Uncle Benson Burchett actually met him at the funeral, in 1911, of Emily Brand (Hamilton's wife) and "got the impression that he was a man with a strong sense of duty and a rather severe code of morals, whose judgments were carefully balanced…[and]… among the last to indulge in any hot-headed act of violence". (There was apparently some garbled family legend at the time that while overseas he had slain a native of India "by way of asserting the respect due to bacon!!!"]

He appears to have died in London in 1911 at the age of 66, [ref. Paddington1a 24, 3rd. quarter]. Rachel is reported to have spent her last years in the Barningham area and had a lych-gate erected in the churchyard in memory of her brother Arthur. There is also a stained glass window in the north side of the nave of the church inscribed: 'In loving memory of William Horne Brand and his wife, Rachel, daughter of Rev. James Edwards rector of this parish.'

The Rev. Hamilton Brand

The youngest child of Charles and Caroline was born in Bath in 1848. While he was still in his infancy, his mother left the family and eloped with a 'lover', leaving Charles with the young children to care for. However, Elizabeth Cecilia, his sister and Hamilton's aunt, stepped into the breach and, at the age of 67, moved down from London to act as a substitute for their mother and is recorded to be living with the family in the census of 1851.

Ten years later, Hamilton is not listed as being in Bath with the family, and probably was away at school by that time, leaving Charles with his daughter, Louisa Georgina, now aged 25, as the lady of the house together with William Horne Brand, aged 16, also recorded as a scholar. No mention of Hamilton has been found elsewhere in the 1861 census yet. By 1871, the family had returned to London to 33, Tavistock Crescent, Paddington, with Charles now listed as 'Retired Commander R.N.', his daughter, Louisa, and son Hamilton, but with no profession or occupation mentioned and, more importantly, no servants recorded.

Charles was to die of bronchitis on May 27 the following year and Hamilton is mentioned as the informant on the death certificate and was awarded probate, but no occupation is given for him at that time.

Charles B's death certificate

1872.

BRAMWELL Jane.
Effects under £300.

22 April.   Administration of the effects of Jane Bramwell late of Holywell in the County of Flint Widow who died 7 January 1872 at Holywell was granted at St. Asaph to Sarah Evans of High-street Holywell Spinster the Sister and one of the Next of Kin.

BRAMWELL Thomas Evans.
Effects under £300.

2 May.   Administration of the effects of Thomas Evans Bramwell late of Holywell in the County of Flint Grocer and Ale and Porter Dealer a Bachelor who died 22 November 1871 at Holywell was granted at St. Asaph to Sarah Evans of High-street Holywell Spinster the Sister and Administratrix of the effects of Jane Bramwell Widow the Mother and only Next of Kin.

BRAN Robert.
Effects under £100.

17 October.   Administration of the effects of Robert Bran late of Lymington in the County of Southampton Publican who died 26 August 1872 at Lymington was granted at Winchester to Celia Bran of Lymington Widow the Relict.

BRANCH Robert.
Effects under £600.

1 November.   The Will of Robert Branch formerly of Wakefield Cottage Goldsmith-road Leyton in the County of Essex but late of Somerset Villa Blenheim-road Deal in the County of Kent Gentleman who died 24 July 1872 at Deal was proved at the Principal Registry by Catherine Sarah Martha Branch of Somerset Villa Widow the Relict the sole Executrix.

BRANCKER { The Reverend Thomas.
Effects under £600.

4 January.   The Will of the Reverend Thomas Brancker late of Limington in the County of Somerset Clerk who died 8 November 1871 at Limington was proved at the Principal Registry by Hannah Brancker of Limington Spinster and Elizabeth Brancker of Limington Spinster the Sisters the Executrixes.

BRAND Charles.
Effects under £200.

14 June.   The Will of Charles Brand late of 33 Tavistock-crescent Westbourne Park in the County of Middlesex a Captain in Her Majesty's Royal Navy who died 27 May 1872 at 33 Tavistock-crescent was proved at the Principal Registry by Hamilton Brand of 33 Tavistock-crescent Gentleman the Son the sole Executor.

BRAND Daniel Patman.
Effects under £100.

7 February.   Administration of the effects of Daniel Patman Brand late of Wallcott near Billinghay in the County of Lincoln Saddler and Publican who died 30 December 1871 at Wallcott was granted at the Principal Registry to Henry Brand of 8 Kidd-street Woolwich in the County of Kent Engineer the Son and one of the Next of Kin.

BRAND Henry.
Effects under £100.

2 August.   Administration of the effects of Henry Brand late of 3 Hoxton-square Hoxton in the County of Middlesex Cabinet Maker who died 6 May 1872 at 3 Hoxton-square was granted at the Principal Registry to Sophia Elizabeth Brand of 3 Hoxton-square Widow the Relict.

157

Charles Brand, probate

Hamilton married Emily Burchett (née Comerford) in about 1873 and, thus acquired a step-son, Benson Burchett, whose later letters to his niece have given much of the anecdotal information about Charles' adventures in Africa and a step-daughter Rosie [ref. Thora Brand's Archive]. By 1881, Hamilton was living in Herne and simply recorded as a 'Gentleman' with his wife, Emily S. Brand, who was 5 years his senior, their sons Digby Hamilton, aged 6, Erle Burgo, 5, Valentine, 3, and step-daughter Rosie Burchett, aged 9.

After this, he attended University College, Durham, where he gained a Licentiate of Theology on 15 December 1885. We are fortunate enough to have a document confirming this, bearing the seal of Durham University.

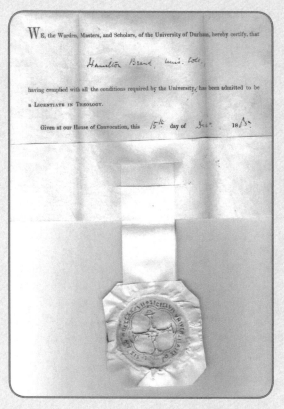

We, the Warden, Masters, and Scholars, of the University of Durham, hereby certify, that

Hamilton Brand, univ. Coll.,

having complied with all the conditions required by the University, has been admitted to be a Licentiate in Theology.

Given at our House of Convocation, this *15th* day of *Dec*ᵗ 18*85*.

Hamilton's Licence in Theology from Durham University

At about this time, Hamilton joined the Church of England priesthood and the census of 1891 finds the family living in Farthingstone, Northants, with Hamilton as Rector of Farthingstone, together with Emily his wife, Rosie Burchett, Digby and Valentine. Erle Burgo was not mentioned so he may have gone to Australia by this time.

Ten years later, Hamilton is still at Farthingstone with Emily and Rosie Burchett, but by this time Digby had left home having gone to America and leaving Valentine at home. Erle Burgo had now returned to England rejoicing in the title of 'Gold Mine Manager' and revealing his place of birth as Burstow, Surrey.

Patrick O'Connor had the pleasure of visiting the former Farthingstone Rectory. In a letter to J. J. B. dated 6 February 1968, my father related that he also had, as a small boy in the early 1900s, stayed on several occasions with his cousins Hamilton and Emily at Farthingstone, when his father, Dr George Henry Brand, was in medical practice in nearby Northampton. Apparently, he did not hear much about Digby or Erle Burgo who had both left home by then while Valentine was kept out of sight because of a disability following an earlier stagecoach accident.

In 1903, the family relocated to Barningham, Norfolk, to St Andrew's Church, which both Patrick O'Connor and J. J. B. have been able to visit in recent years. By courtesy of Robin Comley, there is also now a photo of Hamilton with E. Burgo and his wife, Beatrice, in 1920, when Burgo (aka 'Jack') was awarded his MBE at Buckingham Palace. They appear to have remained there until Hamilton died in 1931, aged 84. Emily had died earlier sometime around 1911, but we have no further information about her except that Uncle Benson attended her funeral, where, as related above, he met Hamilton's brother, William Horne Brand.

Hamilton, 'Jack' and Beatrice, Buckingham Palace,
01.01.1919

And Finally, to Return to Charles Himself

Apparently, he was placed on the reserve list in July 1851 and is described as 'Retired Commander Royal Navy' on 1 July 1861. He obviously returned from Bath to London in the next few years, where, in 1871, he is recorded as living at 33, Tavistock Crescent, Paddington, with his daughter, Louisa Georgina, and son Hamilton. He was probably in retirement by this time, but perhaps was still resident at the same address due to some possible connection with the Canal Company a year later.

He died the following year at the age of 75 on 27 May 1872. His death certificate describes him, perhaps erroneously, as 'Captain, Royal Navy' (unless he had earlier, with the passage of time, enjoyed some kind of promotion) and it states that he died of 'bronchitis'. The informant was his son "Hamilton Brand, present at the death", who, as the sole executor, was granted probate on June 14 for effects of less than £200 [ref. for death cert. from Ancestry. co.uk 2nd. quarter 1872, Kensington 1a Mxx. P.21].

References

1. Naval Biographical Dictionary, O' Byrne J. 1849.

2. Surnames of Scotland, George F. Black, 1946, New York Public Library. The Merry Middies of the Enchantress, Lt. Charles Brand, R.N., 1902, R. A. Everett and Co., London.

3. Thora Brand O'Connor's Archive, A collection of Family Papers and contemporary records [unpublished], Courtesy of Patrick O'Connor, also P.C.'s to J. J. B., 1968.

4. Digby Brand Patagonian Pioneer, Patrick O' Connor, 2006, Lulu Press Inc.

5. The Brands of Baberton, J. John Brand and Muriel P. Brand, 2009, The Scottish Genealogist, Vol. LVI, No. 1.

6. The Fight Against Smuggling Around Eastbourne and Newhaven, Milton, F. R. 1991. Family Roots, FHS., Eastbourne and District.

7. The Diary of Miss Henderson, 1824–1872, Benfleet and District Historical Society.

8. Ghost Ships of the Mersey, Williams, K.J., Countyvise Ltd., Birkenhead, Merseyside.

9. Journal of a Voyage to Peru, Lt. Charles Brand, R.N., 1828, Henry Coleburn, London, now also available as a digitised version from Lulu Books.

Summary

This is the story of the remarkable and adventurous life of a British naval officer at the time of the Napoleonic Wars and after them, in the 19th century. This biography was prepared by Dr J. John Brand, M.D. [Lond.], Surgeon Lt. Cdr. R.N. at the suggestion and with the collaboration of Patrick O'Connor, [Flight Lt. R.A.F.] J. J. B. and P. D. T. O'C. are, in fact, fourth cousins and met quite by accident while they were both working at the RAF Institute of Aviation Medicine, Farnborough, Hants, in 1968. They share common ancestry in Alexander Brand and Ann Rallans and, according to strong family tradition, are descended from the Brand Family of Baberton and Redhall, Edinburgh, Scotland. Charles Brand is great-great-grandfather to P. D. T. O'C. and four times great uncle to J. J. B.

The authors, J.J.B. (left) and P.D.T.O'C.

They discovered their relationship through a chance conversation after a game of squash at Farnborough when Pat mentioned that his mother's maiden name was, in fact, Brand and went on to remark that one of his forebears had made a journey across the Andes on foot in the early 19th century, had written an account of his experiences and wondered if there could be any connection. This sounded like too much of a mere coincidence to J.J.B., who already knew about Charles Brand's journey and subsequent published account. Therefore having been given the appropriate address by Pat, J. J. B. then wrote to Pat's mother, Mrs Thora O'Connor née Brand, then residing in the West Indies, who wrote a friendly reply and, in this way, the relationship was established. Subsequently, both J. J. B. and Pat continued their researches and resulting publications included

'Digby Brand' by Pat in Lulu Press Inc. 2006 and 'The Brands of Baberton' by J. J. B. and M. P. B. in The Scottish Genealogist, 2009.

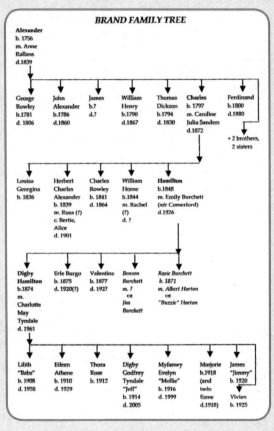

Brand Family Tree (from 'Digby Brand' by Patrick O'Connor)

Regrettably, illness has prevented further closer collaboration since that time.

Part 1. Origins and Early Family Background;

Early Naval Career; The Fight Against the French; the Napoleonic Wars; Defence Against smuggling; St Helena and South Atlantic Station, Adventures in Namaqualand.

Part 2. The Voyage to Peru.

Crossing the Andes on Foot During the Winter of 1828.

Part 3. The Return to England; The Search for Civilian Employment.

Part 4. Marriage in 1834; The Bath Years, Single Parenthood; The Fortunes of His Family.

Part 5. The Children of Charles